Bruce Springsteen:

Biography Of A Great

Artist

By

Amanda Geraldine

Table Of Contents

INTRODUCTION

American singer-songwriter Bruce Frederick Joseph Springsteen was born on September 23, 1949. Throughout a career spanning six decades, he has released 21 studio albums, the majority of which feature his backing band, the E Street Band. He is credited with creating the genre of heartland rock, which combines mainstream rock music with poetic and socially concerned lyrics that depict the lives of Americans in the working class. He is referred to as "The Boss" and is well-known for his rousing concerts that often stretch for more than four hours.

The Wild, the Innocent & the E Street Shuffle
and Greetings from Asbury Park, N.J.,
Springsteen's first two albums, neither of which
were well received, were released in 1973. After
changing his sound, he became a household
name with 1975's Born to Run. Darkness on the
Edge of Town (1978) and The River (1980),
which peaked at number one on the Billboard
200 chart, came after that. He returned with his
E Street Band for Born in the U.S.A. (1984), his
most commercially successful album and one of
the best-selling albums of all time, after
releasing the solo album Nebraska (1982). The
title tune was one of seven of its tracks to make

it into the top 10 on the Billboard Hot 100. For the recording of his following three albums, Tunnel of Love (1987), Human Touch (1992), and Lucky Town (1992), Springsteen primarily used session musicians. He recorded the acoustic album The Ghost of Tom Joad (1995) and the EP Blood Brothers (1996) before reforming the E Street Band for Greatest Hits (1995).

The Rising, which Bruce Springsteen dedicated to the victims of the 9/11 attacks, was released by Springsteen in 2002, seven years after The Ghost of Tom Joad, the longest time between any of his studio albums. He followed up his previous two folk albums with We Shall Overcome: The Seeger Sessions (2006) and Devils & Dust (2005), as well as two additional albums with the E Street Band: Magic (2007) and Working on a Dream (2009). Wrecking Ball (2012) and High Hopes (2014), the following two albums, topped album charts all over the world. Springsteen performed his critically praised one-man play Springsteen on Broadway from 2017 to 2018, and once again in 2021. The show used some of his songs and stories from his 2016 autobiography; the album version was published in 2018. After that, he issued the solo album Western Stars in 2019, the E Street Band's album Letter to You in 2020, and a solo cover album called Only the Strong Survive in 2022. With Letter to You, Springsteen became the first performer to have a top-five album in each of the previous six decades, peaking at No. 2 in the US.

Springsteen, one of the most well-known acts of the album age, has sold more than 71 million records domestically and over 140 million globally, making him one of the best-selling musicians of all time. Twenty Grammy Awards, two Golden Globe Awards, an Academy Award, and a Special Tony Award are just a few of the honors he has received. He received the Kennedy Center Honors in 2009, the MusiCares

Person of the Year award in 2013, the Presidential Medal of Freedom from President Barack Obama in 2016, and the National Medal of Arts from President Joe Biden in 2023. He was also inducted into the Songwriters Hall of Fame and the Rock and Roll Hall of Fame in 1999. He was referred to as "the embodiment of rock & roll" in Rolling Stone's list of the Greatest Artists of All Time, where he was ranked number 23.

CAREER

1964–1972: Early Life And Career Start-up

This was unique and altered the terrain. Four men performed and wrote their music. When rock 'n' roll arrived at my house, there seemed to be no way out, and it unlocked a universe of opportunities.

—Springsteen talking about the Beatles' influence.

Springsteen watched the Beatles' appearances on The Ed Sullivan Show in 1964. Inspiring, he spent $18.95 at the Western Auto appliance store to purchase his first guitar. Following that, he began entertaining crowds with a group called the Rogues at neighborhood venues, including the Elks Lodge in Freehold. Later that year, his mother borrowed money to buy him a $60 Kent guitar; he later paid tribute to this in the song "The Wish".

He visited Tex and Marion Vinyard's home in 1965, who promoted up-and-coming local bands. They assisted him in rising to the position of lead guitarist and later, lead singer, for the Castiles. The band performed at several venues, including Cafe Wha in Greenwich Village, and two original songs were recorded at a public recording studio in Brick Township. Marion Vinyard recalled believing the young Springsteen when he declared he would succeed in the music industry. Late in the 1960s, Springsteen played a few gigs with the power trio Earth in New Jersey bars, with one significant performance at the Hotel Diplomat in New York City.

Springsteen played with the group Child, which eventually went by the name Steel Mill and featured Danny Federici, Vini Lopez, Vinnie Roslin, and later Steve Van Zandt and Robbin Thompson, from 1969 to the beginning of 1971. They frequently gave performances during this time, especially at The Stone Pony on the Jersey Shore. They performed in California, Nashville, Richmond, Virginia, and other cities as well, quickly gaining a cult following. Music writer Philip Elwood's appraisal of their performance at The Matrix in the San Francisco Examiner gave Springsteen early credibility. Elwood praised Steel Mill in his positive review, saying that he had "never been so overwhelmed by an unknown talent" and that the group was "the first big thing that's happened to Asbury Park since the good ship Morro Castle burned to the waterline of that Jersey beach in '34" Elwood continued by praising the band's "cohesive musicality" and specifically referred to Bruce

Springsteen as "a most impressive composer".
Steel Mill used Pacific Recording in San Mateo
to record three of Springsteen's tunes.

Springsteen played with the bands Dr. Zoom &
the Sonic Boom from early to mid-1971, the
Sundance Blues Band in mid-1971, and the
Bruce Springsteen Band from mid-1971 to mid-
1972 while he worked to develop a distinctive
and authentic musical and lyrical approach. His
future record company would say in early
promotional efforts that he had "more words in
some individual songs than other artists had in
whole albums" when describing his prolific
composing talent. He made his abilities known

to various people who would later go on to have a significant impact on the course of his career, including his new managers Mike Appel and Jim Cretecos, who in turn made him known to Columbia Records talent scout John Hammond. In May 1972, Hammond gave Springsteen a test run.

Springsteen put together a new band in October 1972 so they could record his first album, Greetings from Asbury Park, New Jersey. Although the name wasn't used until September 1974, the band eventually became known as the E Street Band. During this time, Springsteen earned the moniker "The Boss" because he took on the responsibility of collecting and sharing the band's nightly pay with his bandmates. According to reports, Springsteen and other Jersey Shore musicians would play Monopoly together, which is where the moniker originated.

1972–1974: The Initial Battle

In 1972, Springsteen was signed to Columbia Records by Clive Davis after catching John Hammond's attention. A decade before, Hammond had brought Bob Dylan to the same label. Springsteen entered the studio with many of his New Jersey-based colleagues and created the E Street Band, despite the Columbia Records executives' hopes that he would record an acoustic album. The band would not be given its official moniker for a few months. Greetings from Asbury Park, New Jersey, his debut album, which was published in January

1973, made him a fan favorite among critics despite its modest sales.

Critics initially connected Springsteen to Dylan because of his lyrical poeticism and folk rock roots, which can be heard on songs like "Blinded by the Light" and "For You," as well as his connections to Columbia and the Hammond organ. In Springsteen's first interview/profile, published in March 1973, Crawdaddy magazine editor Peter Knobler said, "He sings with a freshness and urgency I haven't heard since I was rocked by 'Like a Rolling Stone'." Ed Gallucci took the pictures for the original profile.

Crawdaddy, who was Springsteen's first supporter, discovered him through the rock press. In Crawdaddy, Knobler featured him three times: in 1973, 1975, and 1978. (Springsteen and the E Street Band played a private set at the Crawdaddy 10th Anniversary Party in New York City in June 1976 as a way of thanking the magazine for its support.) When Bruce Springsteen's debut album was released in 1975, "many of us dismissed it: he wrote like Bob Dylan and Van Morrison, sang like Van Morrison and Robbie Robertson, and led a band that sounded like Van Morrison's," noted music reviewer Lester Bangs in Creem.

Springsteen's second studio album, The Wild, the Innocent & the E Street Shuffle, was released in September 1973. Similar to Greetings from Asbury Park, it received favorable reviews but had only little financial success. The E Street Band's less folky, more rhythm and blues-influenced sound let Springsteen's compositions grow in size and scope, and the lyrics frequently idealized adolescent street life. Fans quickly adopted "Incident on 57th Street" and "4th of July, Asbury Park (Sandy)" as favorites, and the protracted, rousing "Rosalita (Come Out Tonight)" is now one of Springsteen's most cherished live songs. As of June 2020, Springsteen had performed "Rosalita" 809 times, making it the eighth most frequently played song in his discography.

In the May 22, 1974, edition of Boston's The Real Paper, music critic Jon Landau penned the following review of Springsteen's performance at the Harvard Square Theater:

"I glimpsed the rock and roll future, and its name is Bruce Springsteen. And on a night when I needed to feel youthful, he gave me the impression that I was only discovering music."

After assisting with the epic new record Born to Run's completion, Landau was hired as Springsteen's manager and producer. Given a sizable budget in a last-ditch attempt to produce a commercially successful album, Springsteen got mired in the recording process while attempting to create a "Wall of Sound" production. However, interest in the album's release grew after his manager, Mike Appel, planned the distribution of an early mix of "Born to Run" to almost a dozen radio stations.

The album took more than 14 months to create, with the song "Born to Run" alone taking six months to produce. Springsteen struggled with rage and irritation over the record at this time, claiming that he heard "sounds in his head" that he was unable to communicate to the other musicians in the studio. On July 13, 1975, while "Tenth Avenue Freeze-Out" was being recorded, Steve Van Zandt was requested to take charge and give the horn players instructions by Bruce Springsteen and Jon Landau. He managed Southside Johnny and the Asbury Jukes, who had the sound they were looking for, and they both knew he played guitar. Each horn player's part was perfectly sung by Van Zandt, who also used flawless time and accent. The horns were recorded, and the musicians performed their parts.

On July 20, the first night of the Born to Run tour, Van Zandt joined the E Street Band. Adding the iconic guitar line to "Born to Run" also assisted Springsteen in making the song even better. Springsteen referred to his friend's contribution to the song's primary riff in the 2005 documentary Wings for Wheels as "arguably Steve's greatest contribution to my music."

On July 25, the album was completed. But Springsteen remained dissatisfied after the long recording sessions. He hurled the final album into the alley when he first heard it, and another master was so terrible that Springsteen threw it out the window of his hotel room and into a river. He informed Appel that he would abandon half of it and replace it with live performances at The Bottom Line in New York City, where he frequently performed.

1975–1983: "Born To Run" And Groundbreaking Success

The Bottom Line club in New York City hosted Bruce Springsteen and the E Street Band for a five-night, ten-show run starting on August 13, 1975. The 10-show run received media coverage and was live-broadcast on WNEW-FM. The stand was cited as one of the "50 Moments That Changed Rock and Roll" by Rolling Stone magazine decades later.

August 25, 1975, saw the release of Born to Run. It turned out to be a ground-breaking record that propelled Springsteen to global fame. The album peaked at No. 3 on the Billboard 200. Although "Born to Run" only reached a modest No. 23 and "Tenth Avenue Freeze-Out" peaked at No. 83 on the Billboard charts, respectively, almost every track on the album received album-oriented rock airplay, especially "Born to Run", "Thunder Road", "Tenth Avenue Freeze-Out", and "Jungleland", all of which are still enduring favorites on much classic rock In the same week in October 1975, Bruce Springsteen was featured on the covers of Newsweek and Time. He eventually revolted against the tsunami of publicity during his first trip abroad by taking down promotional posters before a musical appearance in London since it had grown so enormous.

Springsteen spent over a year away from the recording studio due to a legal dispute with his former manager Mike Appel, but he managed to keep the E Street Band together by doing a lot of traveling around the country.
Although Springsteen frequently performed with an upbeat fervor, his new songs sounded more melancholy than most of his earlier music. After reaching an agreement with Appel in 1977, Springsteen went back to the recording studio, and the ensuing sessions resulted in the 1978 album Darkness on the Edge of Town.

This album marked a turning point in Springsteen's career musically. The previous three albums' songs had lengthy, multi-part musical compositions, outsized characters, and visceral, rapid-fire lyrics; the songs on the fourth album were leaner, more meticulously crafted, and started to represent Springsteen's developing intellectual and political consciousness. The intensity and duration of the 1978 cross-country album promotion tour made it legendary.

Springsteen had a reputation as a songwriter whose work could produce hits for other bands by the late 1970s.

Early in 1977, Manfred Mann's Earth Band released a substantially modified version of Greetings' "Blinded by the Light" that became a U.S. No. 1 pop smash. With updated lyrics, Patti Smith's cover of Bruce Springsteen's unreleased song "Because the Night" peaked at No. 13 in 1978. In 1979, Springsteen's at-the-time unreleased song "Fire" helped The Pointer Sisters reach No. 2. Between 1976 and 1978, Springsteen contributed four songs—including "The Fever" and "Hearts of Stone"—to Southside Johnny & the Asbury Jukes and worked with producer of their first three albums Steven Van Zandt on four more.

In September 1979, Bruce Springsteen and the
E Street Band performed two nights at Madison
Square Garden with the anti-nuclear power
group Musicians United for Safe Energy. They
played a condensed set and debuted two songs
off their upcoming album. Springsteen's
legendary live performance and his first
hesitant foray into politics were captured for
the first time on the ensuing No Nukes live CD
and documentary film, which were released the
following summer.

The 20-song double album The River, released
in 1980, continued Springsteen's focus on

working-class life. It featured a purposefully paradoxical range of songs, from upbeat party rockers to deeply personal ballads, and finally gave rise to "Hungry Heart," his first top-ten hit as a performer. His first Billboard Pop Albums chart No. 1 was achieved thanks to the album's strong sales.

The River and the ominous solo acoustic Nebraska were both released in 1982. Springsteen penned this material when sad, which led to a scathing portrayal of American life, according to Dave Marsh's biographies. Nebraska received enormous critical acclaim, including being awarded "Album of the Year" by the critics of Rolling Stone magazine, and impacted later works by other significant musicians, despite Springsteen's album not selling as well as his previous three.

1984–1986: "Born In The USA" And A Cultural Phenomenon

The album Springsteen is most famous for, Born in the U.S.A. (1984), sold 30 million copies worldwide and 15 million copies in the United States, making it one of the best-selling albums of all time. Seven of its singles also reached the Top 10. The title song was a depressing indictment of how Vietnam veterans—some of whom were Springsteen's friends—were treated. The chorus could be read in a variety of ways, but the lyrics in the verses were difficult for many people, including politicians and the general public, to understand because of the song's anthemic melody and title. As he was fighting for the rights of the average working man, the song had a significant political impact.

The song, which many people mistook for being jingoistic, became a significant part of folklore to the 1984 presidential campaign. After seeing Bruce Springsteen perform in concert in 1984, conservative journalist George Will praised Springsteen's hard ethic in his piece. The president of the United States, Ronald Reagan, declared, "America's future rests in a thousand dreams inside your hearts," at a campaign rally in Hammonton, New Jersey, six days after the essay was published.

"It is rooted in Bruce Springsteen, a native of New Jersey, whose songs carry a message of hope that so many young Americans find inspiring."

—Ronald Reagan confession of Springsteen.

"Well, the president was mentioning my name in his speech the other day and I kind of got to wondering what his favorite album of mine must've been, you know?" Springsteen said to the crowd two nights later at a show in Pittsburgh. "I don't believe the Nebraska album was the cause. He hasn't been listening to this one, I believe. He then started playing "Johnny 99," a song with references to criminals and closed factories."

The most popular of Born in the U.S.A.'s seven hit singles, "Dancing in the Dark" peaked at No. 2 on the Billboard singles list. A young Courteney Cox was shown dancing on stage with Springsteen in the music video, which helped launch the actress's career. Springsteen originally wrote the song "Cover Me" for Donna Summer, but his record company convinced him to save it for the next album. Springsteen, a huge admirer of Summer's work, composed the song "Protection" specifically for her. The album's videos were made by John Sayles and Brian De Palma. In 1985, Springsteen contributed to the song and album "We Are the World". From that album, his live song "Trapped" received average airplay on US Top 40 radio stations and peaked at No. 1 on the Billboard Top Rock Tracks chart.

Due in large part to the release of Arthur Baker's dance mixes of three of the singles, Springsteen's popularity in popular culture reached its peak during the Born in the U.S.A. era. All seven of his albums debuted on the UK Albums Chart from June 15 to August 10, 1985, making him the first artist to simultaneously chart their complete back catalog.

Near the end of 1986, the five-record box set Live/1975-85 (also available on three cassettes or three CDs) was released, becoming the first box set to debut at No. 1 on the U.S. album charts. After selling 13 million copies in the United States, it is one of the best-selling live CDs of all time. Backstreets magazine was among the Springsteen fanzines that were published in the 1980s.

1987–1991: Activism And "The Tunnel Of Love"

In 1987, Springsteen released a lot more somber and reflective Tunnel of Love album. The record, which only seldom employed the E Street Band, is a mature contemplation on the various faces of love discovered, lost, and wasted.

300,000 people attended Bruce Springsteen's concert in East Germany on July 19, 1988. The performance was dubbed "the most important rock concert ever, anywhere" by journalist Erik Kirschbaum in his 2013 book Rocking the Wall;

"Bruce Springsteen: The World-Changing Concert in Berlin."

The Socialist Unity Party's youth section had planned the event to appease East Germany's youth, who yearned for greater freedom and Western pop music. Kirschbaum believes that the concert's success sparked opposition to the East German government and contributed to the fall of the Berlin Wall the following year.

Springsteen was the star of Amnesty International's global Human Rights Now! tour later that year. He disbanded the E Street Band in late 1989.

1992 to 1998: Oscar Winners, Greatest Hits, And Soundtracks

Having moved to Los Angeles and collaborated with studio musicians, Springsteen risked fan allegations of "going Hollywood" by releasing two albums at once in 1992: Human Touch and Lucky Town.

On the acoustic MTV Unplugged television show (later released as In Concert/MTV Plugged), an electric band performance was poorly received and solidified fan discontent. A few years later, during his address accepting him into the Rock and Roll Hall of Fame,

Springsteen seemed to understand this:

What could I have possibly written about without him,

thus I must thank him. You can imagine what might

have happened if everything between us had been

perfect. I tried it in the early 1990s, but it didn't

succeed because the public didn't like it. I would have

only created cheerful songs.

The song "Streets of Philadelphia" by Bruce

Springsteen, which was featured on the

Philadelphia album, was awarded an Academy

Award in 1994. The song's music video features

an instrumental track that has already been recorded and Springsteen's actual vocal performance, which was captured via a hidden microphone. The "Brilliant Disguise" video served as the inspiration for this technique.

The Ghost of Tom Joad, his second folk album, was released in 1995 after he temporarily reorganized the E Street Band for a few new songs recorded for his first Greatest Hits album (a recording session that was documented in the documentary Blood Brothers) and also one show at Tramps in New York City. The Grapes of Wrath by John Steinbeck and Journey to Nowhere: The Saga of the New Underclass, a book by Pulitzer Prize–winning author Dale

Maharidge and photographer Michael

Williamson, served as inspiration for the

album. Due to the minimal melody, twangy

vocals, and political content of the majority of

the songs, the album was largely less well-

received than comparable Nebraska;

nonetheless, some complimented it for giving a

voice to immigrants and other people who

rarely have one in American culture.

Springsteen successfully performed several of

his earlier songs on the extended, international,

small-venue Ghost of Tom Joad Tour that

followed, even though he had to expressly tell

his audiences to "shut the fuck up" and not to applaud during the performances.

After the tour, Springsteen and his family relocated from California to New Jersey. Tracks, a massive four-disc box collection of outtakes, was issued by him in 1998. Later, he would admit that the 1990s were a "lost period" for him, saying, "I didn't accomplish much work. Some might claim that I didn't produce my best work.

1999–2007: The Rising, Devils & Dust, And Other Publications

In 1999, Bono (the lead singer of U2) inducted Bruce Springsteen into the Rock & Roll Hall of Fame; in exchange, Springsteen did the same in 2005.

Springsteen and the E Street Band got back together in 1999 and launched their lengthy Reunion Tour, which lasted for more than a year. Highlights included a record-breaking 15-show run at the East Rutherford, New Jersey's Continental Airlines Arena, and a ten-night engagement at Madison Square Garden in New

York City, all of which were sold out. At these concerts, a brand-new song about Amadou Diallo's police shooting, "American Skin (41 Shots)," caused controversy.

The Rising, which was produced by Brendan O'Brien, was Springsteen's 2002 studio album and the first in 18 years to feature the entire band. The album, which mostly addressed the September 11 attacks, was well-received by critics and listeners alike. The album's title tune received rotation on various radio stations, and it went on to become Springsteen's best-selling new music album in 15 years. The Rising Tour began with an early morning performance by Asbury Park on The Today Show, and the group then barnstormed their way through a string of one-night arena shows around the United States and Europe. In New Jersey's Giants Stadium, Springsteen performed for ten nights straight, a record. The Rising was nominated for Album of the Year and won the Grammy for Best Rock Album at the 45th Annual Grammy Awards. "The Rising" also took home awards for Best Male Rock Vocal Performance and Best Rock Song. Additionally, it was a nominee for Song of the Year at the Grammy Awards. Later, "The Rising" was ranked as the 35th best song of the decade by

Rolling Stone. The "100 Greatest Songs of the '00s" list compiled by VH1 ranked it 81st.

In 2003, Springsteen paid tribute to Joe Strummer at the Grammy Awards by performing "London Calling" by the Clash alongside Elvis Costello, Dave Grohl, Steven Van Zandt of the E Street Band, and Tony Kanal, the bassist of No Doubt. In 2004, John Mellencamp, John Fogerty, the Dixie Chicks, Pearl Jam, R.E.M., Bright Eyes, the Dave Matthews Band, Jackson Browne, and other musicians took part in the Vote for Change tour with Bruce Springsteen and the E Street Band.

On April 26, 2005, Devils & Dust was made

public. It was not produced by the E Street

Band. Similar to Nebraska and The Ghost of

Tom Joad, it is a subdued, primarily acoustic

record. Some of the songs were written during

or shortly after the Ghost of Tom Joad Tour,

almost ten years prior. A few were even

performed but not recorded at the time. The

title track explores the emotions and worries of

a regular soldier during the Iraq War. In ten

nations, the album debuted at the top of the

charts. At the same time as the album's release,

Springsteen launched his solo Devils & Dust

Tour, performing in both intimate and

expansive settings. In some areas, the turnout was underwhelming, and elsewhere (apart from in Europe), tickets were easier to get by than in the past.

We Shall Overcome: The Seeger Sessions, an American roots music project centered around a huge folk sound treatment of 15 songs made known by Pete Seeger's radical musical activism, was released by Bruce Springsteen in April 2006. The 18-piece band, known as the Seeger Sessions Band (later abbreviated to the Sessions Band), started a tour that same month. The tour was extremely successful in Europe, selling out every event and garnering some great reviews, but newspapers claimed that a number of the U.S. performances were plagued by low turnout.

Magic, Springsteen's subsequent album, was made available on October 2, 2007. It was recorded with the E Street Band and featured 10 brand-new Springsteen songs, plus "Long Walk Home," which was once performed with the Sessions band, and "Terry's Song," a secret track that was the first to be included on a Springsteen studio album in memory of Springsteen's longtime assistant Terry Magovern, who passed away on July 30, 2007. In both Ireland and the UK, Magic debuted at No. 1.

On November 21, 2007, it was revealed that Danny Federici, Springsteen's longtime friend and a founding member of the E Street Band, would be taking a break from the Magic Tour to pursue melanoma treatment. Federici was relieved and Charles Giordano took his position.

2008–2011: Political Engagement, The Super Bowl XLIII, And Kennedy Center Honors

On March 20, 2008, Federici took the stage once more for a Springsteen and E Street Band show in Indianapolis. Cancer claimed Federici's life on April 17, 2008.

Springsteen backed Barack Obama's election campaign in 2008. Throughout 2008, he gave solo acoustic performances in support of Obama's campaign, coming to a head on November 2 at a rally where he made his song "Working on a Dream" debut in a duet with

Scialfa. After Obama's victory speech in Chicago's Grant Park on November 4, Springsteen's song "The Rising" was the first to be played over the loudspeakers. Over 400,000 people attended the Obama Inaugural Celebration on January 18, 2009, which featured Springsteen as the musical opener. He sang "The Rising" with a choir made up entirely of women. Later, he and Pete Seeger performed "This Land Is Your Land" by Woody Guthrie.

Springsteen received the Golden Globe for Best Song for "The Wrestler" from the Darren Aronofsky movie of the same name on January 11, 2009. Springsteen gave the movie's theme tune away after getting a touching letter from star Mickey Rourke.

On February 1, 2009, Springsteen agreed to play for the halftime show of Super Bowl XLIII after previously declining. Springsteen held a rare press conference a few days before the game, promising a "twelve-minute party." According to reports, Springsteen's news conference was his first in more than 25 years. With the E Street Band and the Miami Horns, he performed a 12-minute 45-second set that comprised shortened versions of "Tenth Avenue Freeze-Out," "Born to Run," "Working on a Dream," and "Glory Days," the latter of which featured football references in place of the song's original baseball-themed lyrics. This has certainly been the busiest month of my life, Springsteen said about the array of engagements and promotional efforts.

Danny Federici's memory was honored with the publication of Bruce Springsteen's album Working on a Dream in late January 2009. From April 2009 through November 2009, the supporting Working on a Dream Tour was in operation. The band played five last gigs at Giants Stadium, starting each one with "Wrecking Ball," a new song that included the iconic stadium and Springsteen's New Jersey background. London Calling: Live in Hyde Park, a DVD from the Working on a Dream Tour, was released in 2010.

On December 6, 2009, Springsteen received the Kennedy Center Honors. In a speech, President Obama claimed that Bruce Springsteen had incorporated everyday Americans' lives into his diverse catalog of songs. Obama further stated that Springsteen's performances were "communions" rather than merely rock and roll events. Melissa Etheridge, Ben Harper, John Mellencamp, Jennifer Nettles, Sting, and Eddie Vedder performed musical tributes at the occasion.

With Springsteen's tours placing him fourth among musicians in terms of overall concert receipts for the decade, the 2000s came to a close with him being named one of Rolling Stone magazine's eight musicians of the Decade.

The founding member and saxophonist of the E Street Band, Clarence Clemons, passed away on June 18, 2011, as a result of complications from a stroke.

2012–2018: Autobiography And A Broadway Production

Wrecking Ball, Springsteen's 17th studio album was released on March 6, 2012. Eleven songs and two additional tracks make up the album. The CD includes the live versions of three songs, including "Wrecking Ball," "Land of Hope and Dreams," and "American Land." Springsteen tied Elvis Presley for the third-most No. 1 albums of all time with Wrecking Ball, his tenth No. 1 album in the US. With more No. 1 albums, only the Beatles (19) and Jay Z (12) have more.

Springsteen and the E Street Band made arrangements for the Wrecking Ball Tour after the album's release, which kicked off on March 18, 2012. Springsteen gave his longest concert ever on July 31, 2012, in Helsinki, Finland, lasting 4 hours, and 6 minutes, and featuring 33 songs.

In Ohio, Iowa, Virginia, Pittsburgh, and Wisconsin, Springsteen ran a re-election campaign for President Barack Obama. He gave a brief speech to the crowd and played a small acoustic set at the rallies, which included the freshly penned song "Forward."

The Wrecking Ball Tour won the Billboard Touring Awards' Top Draw award for having the highest attendance of any tour at the end of the year. Compared to Roger Waters, who had the highest-grossing tour of 2012, the tour came in second. With $33.44 million, Springsteen was the second-highest earner in 2012, trailing only Madonna. Three Grammy Awards, including Best Rock Performance, Best Rock Song for "We Take Care of Our Own," and Best Rock Album, were nominated for the Wrecking Ball album and the song "We Take Care of Our Own". On their list of the Top 50 albums of 2012, Rolling Stone ranked Wrecking Ball as the best album of the year.

The documentary Springsteen & I, which was produced and directed by Ridley Scott and Bailie Walsh, was simultaneously shown in over 2000 theaters and over 50 countries as part of a global cinema broadcast in late July 2013.

High Hopes, Springsteen's 18th studio album, was made available on January 14, 2014. A brand-new recording of the 1995 Springsteen song "High Hopes" served as the album's first single and music video. It was Springsteen's first album in which every song was either a cover, an outtake from an earlier record, or a newly recorded version of a previously released song. The CD features the 2014 E Street Band touring lineup as well as dead E Street Band members Danny Federici and Clarence Clemons. High Hopes became Bruce Springsteen's 11th US No. 1 album. It was his tenth UK No. 1, tying him with the Rolling Stones and U2 for fifth place all-time. On their list of the Top 50 Albums of 2014, Rolling Stone ranked High Hopes as the second-best album of the year, just behind Songs of Innocence by U2.

In the season three finale of Van Zandt's television series Lilyhammer, titled "Loose Ends" after one of Springsteen's songs from the album Tracks, he made his acting debut.

In honor of Stewart's final "Moment of Zen,"
Springsteen sang "Born to Run" and "Land of
Hope and Dreams" on the final episode of The
Daily Show with Jon Stewart on August 6, 2015.
Springsteen launched The Ties That Bind: The
River Collection box set on October 16 to mark
the 35th anniversary of The River. It was
released on December 4 and includes a 148-
page coffee table book, three DVDs (or Blu-ray),
four CDs (several of which feature previously
unreleased tracks), and three DVDs. "American
Skin (41 Shots)" was played at Shining a Light:
A Concert for Progress on Race in America in
November 2015 alongside John Legend. On

December 19, 2015, Springsteen performed "Meet Me in the City," "The Ties That Bind," and "Santa Claus Is Coming to Town" on Saturday Night Live for the first time since 2002.

In promotion of the box set The Ties That Bind: The River Collection, the River Tour 2016 got underway in January 2016. The River album was performed in its entirety, along with other songs from Springsteen's discography, at every first-leg concert in North America. Each performance was recorded and made available for purchase. Springsteen was among the first musicians to boycott North Carolina's anti-transgender bathroom law in April 2016. Later, additional dates were revealed, turning the initial three-month tour into a seven-month journey that included performances in Europe in May 2016 and a second North American leg that began in August 2016 and concluded the following month.

Chapter & Verse, a collection of songs from Springsteen's whole career stretching back to 1966, was published on September 23, 2016. Simon & Schuster released his 500-page autobiography, Born to Run, on September 27, 2016. The book swiftly ascended to the top of the New York Times Best Sellers List.

Springsteen gave a 4-hour, 4-minute set on September 7, 2016, at Citizens Bank Park in Philadelphia, Pennsylvania. His longest performance in the United States to date was this one, which was a stop on The River 2016 Tour. The River 2016 Tour was the highest-grossing international tour of 2016, bringing in $268.3 million worldwide. It surpassed Taylor Swift's 2015 tour, which brought in $250.1 million.

At a rally in Philadelphia on November 7, 2016, Springsteen gave an acoustic performance of "Thunder Road," "Long Walk Home," and

"Dancing in the Dark" in support of Hillary Clinton's 2016 presidential campaign. Barack Obama gave Bruce Springsteen the Presidential Medal of Freedom on November 22, 2016. Two days before President Barack Obama's farewell address to the country, on January 12, 2017, Springsteen and Patti Scialfa conducted a special 15-song acoustic set for the Obamas in the East Room of the White House.

In the fall of 2017, Springsteen on Broadway, an eight-week run at the Walter Kerr Theatre on Broadway in New York City, will go on. In addition to delivering other spoken memories, Springsteen read passages from his 2016 autobiography Born to Run during the performance. The show's first run was supposed to span from October 12 through November 26, but it was three times extended; its final performance took place on December 15, 2018. At the 72nd Tony Awards in 2018, Springsteen received a Special Tony Award for his Broadway production of Springsteen.

Springsteen on Broadway, a live CD, was released on December 14th, 2018. The album peaked at no. 10 in the United States and no. 10 in more than ten other nations.

2019–2023: Continuing Success

Western Stars, Springsteen's twentieth studio album, was released on June 14, 2019.

The Toronto Film Festival will have Springsteen's Western Stars premiere in September 2019, it was announced on July 23, 2019. Together with his longtime business partner Thom Zimny, he co-directed the movie. The soundtrack from Western Stars is performed live on-screen by Springsteen and his supporting band. The movie's soundtrack, Western Stars - Songs from the Film, was also released on October 25, 2019, the same day it was released in theaters.

On May 29, 2020, Springsteen made a virtual appearance at Fenway Park in Boston Fenway Park during a Dropkick Murphys streaming performance with no audience. Together with Ken Casey, Springsteen sang co-vocals on the Dropkick Murphys song "Rose Tattoo" and his song "American Land" during the performances. The occasion marked the first music performance at a significant American arena, stadium, or ballpark without an actual audience during the COVID-19 epidemic. Viewers were urged to give to charity while the stream was live. Over 9 million people watched the live stream, which raised over $70,000.

Springsteen released the song "Letter to You" on September 10, 2020. On September 24, 2020, the song "Ghosts" was made available. On October 23, 2020, Springsteen's twenty-first studio album, Letter to You, was made available. On October 23, Springsteen also made a documentary titled Letter to You. Thom Zimny was the director of the documentary, which was entirely captured in black and white. The 12 songs on the album Letter to You total a little under an hour in length.

For the third studio album "Take the Sadness Out of Saturday Night", Bleachers' newest single, "Chinatown," was released on November 16, 2020, and it featured Springsteen as a guest singer.

On the episode of Saturday Night Live airing on December 12, 2020, Springsteen and the E Street Band performed "Ghosts" and "I'll See You in My Dreams" as musical guests. The group's first performance since 2017 and their first to support Letter to You was this one. Due to concerns about COVID-19, Garry Tallent and Soozie Tyrell decided to stay at home. This was the first time Tallent had ever missed a performance with the band, and Jack Daley of the Disciples of Soul filled in.

On February 22, 2021, news of Bruce Springsteen's eight-part podcast series Renegades: Born in the USA was released. It would feature Springsteen and Barack Obama conversing about a range of subjects, including family, race, marriage, fatherhood, and the state of the United States.

John Mellencamp revealed that Bruce Springsteen would be a part of his upcoming album on May 16, 2021. Mellencamp's "Wasted Days" song and music video, which includes

Springsteen on co-lead vocals and guitar, were released on September 29, 2021.

Springsteen revealed on June 7, 2021, that his Springsteen on Broadway performances would make a brief comeback at Jujamcyn's St. James Theatre starting on June 26, 2021. Springsteen stated that he had no intention of performing live in 2021 but had been persuaded to take the stage for the Broadway productions by a "friend" in an interview with Jim Rotolo of E Street Radio on June 10, 2021. Springsteen disclosed a future collaboration with the Killers in the same interview. The Killers teased the song's title throughout the day, and later that day, "Dustland" was officially revealed on their social media accounts.

In remembrance of the victims of the September 11 attacks, Bruce Springsteen played "I'll See You in My Dreams" on September 11, 2021.

Steve Earle and the Dukes joined Bruce Springsteen on stage for a surprise four-song set on December 13, 2021, as part of the John Henry's Friends benefit event for youngsters with autism. By saying, "Until the bus pulls up at my house, figuratively speaking, I'm not quite sure but I'm pretty convinced... (that) myself, my colleagues, and the people who are interested are going to be very pleasantly surprised in 2022," Max Weinberg said on December 14, 2021, he felt that a tour with Springsteen and the E Street Band was very likely in 2022. "Bruce Springsteen and the E Street Band are not on my calendar, but I have high hopes for the upcoming 18 to 24 months."

Springsteen paid $500 million to Sony Music on December 16, 2021, in exchange for the master recordings of his entire discography as well as the corresponding publishing rights. This was $200 million more than what Taylor Swift and Bob Dylan were paid for their catalogs. He was ranked first on the Rolling Stone list of the

highest-paid musicians of 2021 thanks to this

transaction as well as his Broadway

performances and collaborations with Obama.

 On May 24, 2022, it was revealed that he would

embark on the E Street Band's first world tour

since 2017 in 2023.

Springsteen and his wife Patti Scialfa will

perform at the first-ever Albie Awards on

September 29, 2022, at the New York Public

Library, which was announced on September

26, 2022.

Springsteen declared on September 29, 2022, that the release date of his twenty-first studio album, Only the Strong Survive, would be November 11, 2022. 15 iconic soul songs from the 1960s and 1970s are covered on the album, which was preceded by the singles "Do I Love You (Indeed I Do)," "Nightshift," "Don't Play That Song," and "Turn Back the Hands of Time." Springsteen played on The Tonight Show Starring Jimmy Fallon on November 14, 15, and 16, 2022, as well as a special Thanksgiving episode on November 24, all to promote the album.

PRIVATE LIFE

Relationships

Early in the 1980s, Springsteen had a four-year
relationship with actress Joyce Hyser. He
previously dated models Karen Darvin and
Lynn Goldsmith, a photographer. He first ran
with Patti Scialfa at The Stone Pony in New
Jersey in the early 1980s while she was
performing with Bobby Bandiera, a buddy with
whom she had co-written the song "At Least
We Got Shoes" for Southside Johnny. After the
concert, Springsteen approached her because

he thought she had a good voice. They quickly began spending time together and grew close.

Springsteen invited Scialfa to join the E Street Band for the impending Born in the U.S.A. Tour in the early months of 1984. They appeared to be dating during the first leg of the tour, according to Peter Ames Carlin's book Bruce, but on May 13, 1985, just after midnight, Springsteen married actress Julianne Phillips at Our Lady of the Lake Catholic Church in Lake Oswego, Oregon. The two were opposites with an 11-year age gap, and Springsteen's touring hurt their bond. On his album Tunnel of Love, he wrote numerous songs that expressed his unhappiness with Phillips. Late in February

1988, Springsteen persuaded Scialfa to rejoin

the Tunnel of Love Express Tour. Initially

hesitant to join the tour because she wanted to

begin recording her debut solo album, she

eventually agreed to do so after hearing that it

would only be a brief stopover. Springsteen and

Phillips split up in the spring of 1988, but it was

kept a secret. During the Tunnel of Love

Express Tour, Springsteen and Scialfa fell in

love, and soon after his split from Phillips, they

moved in together. On August 30, 1988, Phillips

filed for divorce in Los Angeles, citing

irreconcilable differences. A settlement was

made in December, and the divorce was then

formalized on March 1, 1989. They didn't have any kids.

Springsteen faced backlash from the media for what appeared to be his and Scialfa's hurried courtship. He described the subsequent negative press the couple received to Judy Wieder in a 1995 interview with The Advocate, saying, "It's a bizarre society that feels it has the right to tell individuals whom they should love and whom they shouldn't. However, the truth is that I did my best to ignore everything about it."

"Well, all I know is that this feels real, and perhaps I've got a mess on my hands here in some way, but that's life. Some type of public declaration would have been reasonable, but I felt unduly concerned about my privacy, he later recalled. "I didn't safeguard Juli,' he said years later. I handled it poorly, and I'm still unhappy with myself. People learning the information in the manner they did was harsh."

Before relocating to Los Angeles, where they intended to conceive a family, Springsteen and Scialfa lived in New Jersey. Evan James Springsteen, the couple's first child, was born on July 25, 1990, thanks to Scialfa. Springsteen and Scialfa exchanged vows in a private ceremony on June 8, 1991, at their home in Los

Angeles, in front of only their immediate family and close friends. On December 30, 1991, Jessica Rae Springsteen, their second child, was born. Samuel Ryan Springsteen, their third child, was born on January 5th, 1994.

"I went through a divorce, and it was really difficult and painful, and I was very afraid about getting married again," Springsteen remarked in a 1995 interview. "Therefore, a part of me questioned, 'What does it matter?' But it is significant. It's significantly different than simply cohabitating. First and foremost, assuming a public role is something you do when you obtain your license and participate in other social rituals. This is a component of your place in society and contributes in some way to society's approval of you. I discovered that it did have meaning, as did Patti."

Springsteen and Scialfa relocated back to New Jersey in the 1990s when their kids started school so they could raise them away from the media. The family also owns mansions in Rumson, Los Angeles, and Wellington, Florida. They also own a horse farm in Colts Neck Township, where they reside. Evan, a Boston College alumnus, is a self-taught songwriter and performer who took first place in the 2012 Singer/Songwriter Competition at the Boston

College Arts Festival. Jessica is a champion equestrian who attended Duke University and graduated. In August 2014, she made her show-jumping debut while competing for Team USA. Sam works as a Jersey City firefighter.

When Sam and his fiancée had a daughter on July 17, 2022, Springsteen and Scialfa became grandparents for the first time.

Health

Springsteen has lived a drug-free existence throughout his whole life. Steven Van Zandt, Bruce Springsteen's longtime bandmate, remarked in 2012 that "Springsteen is the only guy I know—I think the only guy I know at all—who never did drugs." He has discussed his battles with depression, which he only started talking about in his 30s after years of denial. He started eating largely vegetarian, ran up to six miles on the treadmill, and worked out three times a week after becoming upset with being an underweight "fast food junkie" who needed assistance leaving the stage after a performance. According to a 2019 Consequence

story honoring his 70th birthday, he still

follows this routine and diet.

Views

Springsteen admitted in his 2016 autobiography
Born to Run that he has a "personal
relationship with Jesus" despite first rejecting
religion. I have faith in God's ability to save, to
love, but not to damn. He has said that he
"came to ruefully and bemusedly understand
that once you're a Catholic you're always a
Catholic" about his lapsed Catholicism. "I don't
practice my religion, but I know deep down
that I'm still on the team", he continued.,

Springsteen acknowledged being a tax evader
early in his career in a 2017 interview with Tom

Hanks. He claimed that the government did not pay much attention to his taxes until he was featured on the cover of Time magazine in 1975. Even though he had several top-selling records and sold-out tours, almost all of his money over the following several years went toward paying back his taxes, leaving him with barely $20,000 by the time he was 30.

Politics

Springsteen announced his support for Barack Obama's 2008 candidacy for president in April 2008. Throughout 2008, he made several appearances at rallies in support of Obama's campaign. Springsteen spoke at a rally in Ohio about the value of "truth, transparency, and integrity in government, the right of every American to have a job, a living wage, to receive a decent education and a life filled with the dignity of work, the promise, and the sanctity of the home." Springsteen is featured on card #59, "the 'O' Street Band," in the commemorative trading card set released by

Topps to celebrate the support. Springsteen supported Obama's re-election in Ohio, Iowa, Virginia, Pittsburgh, and Wisconsin after declaring he would skip the 2012 presidential contest.

Springsteen is a vocal advocate for LGBT rights and has frequently expressed his support for gay marriage. He discussed the significance of gay marriage in an April 1996 interview with The Advocate, saying:

"You get your license, you complete all the social rites. It contributes to your social standing and, in certain ways, to society's acceptance of you."

He wrote on his website in 2009,

"I've long believed in and have always spoken out for the rights of same-sex couples and fully agree with Governor Corzine when he writes that 'The marriage-equality issue should be recognized for what it truly is–a civil rights issue that must be approved to assure that every citizen is treated equally under the law.'"

He provided his support to the "The Four 2012" campaign, which promoted gay marriage, in 2012. "I couldn't agree more with that statement," stated Springsteen in the advertisement. "I urge those who support equal treatment for our gay and lesbian brothers and sisters to let their voices be heard now." Days before it was scheduled to take place, in April 2016, Bruce Springsteen canceled a concert in Greensboro, North Carolina, in protest of the city's recently enacted Public Facilities Privacy & Security Act, also known as the "bathroom law," which limits which restrooms transgender people are allowed to use and bars LGBT people from bringing legal action for workplace discrimination. On his website, Springsteen posted a formal statement. Springsteen's statement was applauded by the Human Rights Campaign, and the LGBT community expressed their love and admiration for him.

Springsteen made the following statement while performing in Perth, Australia, in 2017:

"We're a long way from home, and our hearts and spirits are with the hundreds of thousands of women and men who marched yesterday in every city in America, and in Melbourne... They demonstrated support for tolerance, inclusion, racial justice, LGBTQ rights, the environment, pay equality, gender equality, healthcare, and immigrant rights as well as against

hatred and division. We support you. The modern

American resistance is ourselves."

Throughout Trump's presidency, Springsteen was a vocal opponent of the president. In June 2020, he referred to Trump as a "threat to our democracy," while in October 2019, he claimed that Trump "doesn't have a grasp of the deep meaning of what it means to be an American." With a new video and the hashtag #TheRising, Springsteen's song "The Rising" was prominently played during the 2020 Democratic National Convention to support Joe Biden. Before Trump's campaign event in Pennsylvania on October 13, 2020, author Don

Winslow put out a video in which he criticized the president. "Streets of Philadelphia" by Bruce Springsteen is included in the video. Springsteen gave a voiceover for a campaign ad that highlights Biden's background in Scranton, Pennsylvania, a few days before the 2020 US presidential election, with "My Hometown" playing throughout the ad. As Obama had done before him in 2012, Biden used "We Take Care of Our Own" as one of his theme songs.

TALENT AND LEGACY

I measured the gap between the American Dream and American reality throughout most of my time as a musician.

—Springsteen on November 2, 2008, at a rally in support of Barack Obama for president.

Springsteen, who is recognized as one of history's greatest composers, has been dubbed a "rock 'n' roll poet" who "radiates working-class authenticity." His creative output "epitomizes rock's deepest values: desire, the need for freedom, and the search to find yourself."

Springsteen's songs usually tackle deeply

personal topics like individual dedication,

unhappiness, and dismay with life in the

context of commonplace occurrences. They are

frequently described as cinematic in scope. The

challenges that Springsteen's own family of

origin encountered serve as the foundation for

his themes, which often incorporate social and

political commentary.

Born to Run (18), Born in the U.S.A. (85), The

Wild, the Innocent & the E Street Shuffle (132),

Darkness on the Edge of Town (151), Nebraska

(224), The River (250), Greetings from Asbury

Park, N.J. (379), and Tunnel of Love (475) were

all on Rolling Stone's list of the 500 Greatest Albums of All Time in 2003. In 2004, Rolling Stone included "Born to Run" (number 21), "Thunder Road" (number 86), and "Born in the USA" (number 275) among the 500 Greatest Songs of All Time. He is ranked as the sixth most renowned musician in the history of popular music by Acclaimed Music.

With the release of the album Darkness on the Edge of Town, Springsteen's lyrical style changed as he began to emphasize the emotional struggles of working-class life in addition to more conventional rock and roll themes. Debby Miller, a Rolling Stone writer, wrote in her review of Bruce Springsteen's Born in the U.S.A. album that Springsteen "ignored the British Invasion and embraced instead the legacy of Phil Spector's releases, the kind of soul that was coming from Atlantic Records, and especially the garage bands that had anomalous radio hits." He has long sought after that music's utopian feeling.

Springsteen was listed in the "pantheon" of album-era musicians by Jon Pareles. While artists like the Beatles, Rolling Stones, and Marvin Gaye may have created better individual works, according to Ann Powers, "none had used the long-player form itself more powerfully over the arc of a career, not only to establish a world through the song but to inhabit an enduring persona. Springsteen is the quintessential album-era rock star." He lyricized "America's slide from industrial-era swagger into service-economy anomie" using it. Springsteen, in her opinion, needs the "track-by-track architecture of albums to flesh out characters, relate each to the other, extend metaphors and build a palpable, detail-filled landscape through which they could travel." He developed musically at the same time, "both with his stalwart E Street Band (a metaphor itself for the family connections and community spirit his songs celebrate or lament)

and in more minimalist projects."

The fact that Bruce Springsteen appears to be
booed by his fans when he takes the stage
frequently confuses concertgoers. His name is
being yelled out by his fans as "Bruuuce,"
which sounds like boos.

Via April 2023, the New Jersey governor
declared September 23 to be "Bruce
Springsteen Day" via a proclamation.

Awards, Nominations, And Accomplishments

One of the best-selling musicians in the world, Springsteen has sold more than 140 million records globally including more than 71 million in the United States. Twenty Grammy Awards, two Golden Globe Awards, an Academy Award, and a Special Tony Award (for Springsteen on Broadway) are just a few of the accolades he has received for his work.

In addition to receiving the Kennedy Center Honors in 2009, MusiCares Person of the Year in 2013, and the Presidential Medal of Freedom from President Barack Obama in 2016,

Springsteen was inducted into the Songwriters Hall of Fame and the Rock & Roll Hall of Fame in 1999. The Woody Guthrie Prize, awarded in May 2021 to an artist who promotes social justice and upholds the folk singer's spirit, made Bruce Springsteen the ninth recipient.

President Joe Biden presented Bruce Springsteen with the 2021 National Medal of Arts in March 2023 at the White House. The COVID-19 epidemic forced the postponement of the celebrations, which were intended to take place in 2021 and honor Springsteen.

DISCOGRAPHY

Studio Albums

- Greetings from Asbury Park, N.J. (1973)

- The Wild, the Innocent & the E Street Shuffle (1973)

- Born to Run (1975)

- Darkness on the Edge of Town (1978)

- The River (1980)

- Nebraska (1982)

- Born in the U.S.A. (1984)

- Tunnel of Love (1987)

- Human Touch (1992)

- Lucky Town (1992)

- The Ghost of Tom Joad (1995)

- The Rising (2002)

- Devils & Dust (2005)

- We Shall Overcome: The Seeger Sessions (2006)

- Magic (2007)

- Working on a Dream (2009)

- Wrecking Ball (2012)

- High Hopes (2014)

- Western Stars (2019)

- Letter to You (2020)

- Only the Strong Survive (2022)

- Concert tours

Tours

Springsteen has developed a reputation for energetic and long-lasting live performances.

Headlining Tours

- Born to Run tours (1974–1977)

- Darkness Tour (1978–1979)

- The River Tour (1980–1981)

- Born in the U.S.A. Tour (1984–1985)

- Tunnel of Love Express Tour (1988)

- Bruce Springsteen 1992–1993 World Tour (1992–1993)

- Ghost of Tom Joad Tour (1995–1997)

- Bruce Springsteen and the E Street Band Reunion Tour (1999–2000)
- The Rising Tour (2002–2003)
- Devils & Dust Tour (2005)
- Bruce Springsteen with the Seeger Sessions Band Tour (2006)
- Magic Tour (2007–2008)
- Working on a Dream Tour (2009)
- Wrecking Ball World Tour (2012–2013)
- High Hopes Tour (2014)
- The River Tour (2016–2017)
- Springsteen on Broadway (2017–2018, 2021)
- 2023 Tour (2023)

Co-headlining Tours

- Human Rights Now! (1988)
- Vote for Change (2004)

Printed in Great Britain
by Amazon

33020857R00066